P9-BIN-497

Erin Pembrey Swan

Meat-eating Marsupials

Franklin Watts - A Division of Scholastic Inc.
New York • Toronto • London • Auckland • Sydney
New Mexico • New Delhi • Hong Kong
Danbury, Connecticut

For Jason

Photographs ©: Animals Animals: 42 (Hans & Judy Beste), 5 top right (Breck P. Kent), 1 (A. Wells/OSF); Auscape: 5 bottom left (Kathie Atkinson), cover, 7, 19, 39 (Jean-Paul Ferrero), 41 (Ian D. Goodwin), 17, 40 (Greg Harold), 6, 22, 23, 30, 31 (C. Andrew Henley), 15, 29 (Reg Morrison), 26, 27, 36, 37 (D. Parer & E. Parer-Cook); BBC Natural History Unit/John Cancalosi: 5 top left; NHPA/Martin Harvey: 33; Peter Arnold Inc.: 20, 21 (Doug Cheeseman), 5 bottom right, 25 (Roland Seitre); Photo Researchers, NY: 12, 13 (Bill Bachman) 35, 43 (Tom McHugh).

Illustrations by Pedro Julio Gonzalez and Steve Savage

The photo on the cover shows a mulgara eating an insect. The photo on the title page shows a fat-tailed dunnart with her babies.

Library of Congress Cataloging-in-Publication Data

Swan, Erin Pembrey.
    Meat-eating marsupials / Erin Pembrey Swan
    p. cm. — (Animals in order)
    Includes bibliographical references and index.
    ISBN 0-531-11628-X (lib. bdg.)
    I. Dasyuromorphia—Juvenile literature. [1. Marsupials.] I. Gonzalez, Pedro Julio, ill. II. Savage, Stephen, 1965-ill. III. Title. IV. Series.
QL737.M325 S82   2001
599.2'7—dc21
                                                                                              2001017956

Contents

What Is a Meat-eating Marsupial? - 4
Traits of Meat-eating Marsupials - 6
The Order of Living Things - 8
How Meat-eating Marsupials Fit In - 10

MEAT-EATING MARSUPIALS IN FORESTS

Numbat - 12
Tiger Quoll - 14
Southern Dibbler - 16
Brush-tailed Phascogale - 18

Tasmanian Devil - 20
Dusky Antechinus - 22
Chuditch - 24

MEAT-EATING MARSUPIALS IN FORESTS AND GRASSLANDS

Tasmanian Wolf - 26   Fat-tailed Dunnart - 28   Eastern Quoll - 30

MEAT-EATING MARSUPIALS IN DESERTS AND GRASSLANDS

Mulgara - 32   Kultarr - 34   Kowari - 36

MEAT-EATING MARSUPIALS IN ROCKY PLAINS

Little Northern Native Cat - 38

Meat-eating Marsupials and People - 40
Words to Know - 44
Learning More - 46
Index - 47

What Is a Meat-eating Marsupial?

What is as tiny as a grain of rice when it is born, begins its life in a fold of skin, and grows up to eat other animals? The answer to this riddle is the name of some very important animals. Give up? They are meat-eating *marsupials*—marsupials that eat meat instead of plants.

There are other kinds of marsupials, such as kangaroos, opossums, and koalas. But they do not eat meat, and they belong to a different group, or *order*, of animals. Meat-eating marsupials belong to the order called *dasyuromorphia* (dazz-yer-oh-MORE-fee-uh).

Three of the animals shown on the next page are meat-eating marsupials. One of them is not. Can you guess which one is *not* a meat-eating marsupial?

Tasmanian devil

Deer mouse

Mulgara

Numbat

Traits of Meat-eating Marsupials

Did you guess the deer mouse? You were right! How could you tell it is not a meat-eating marsupial?

Although many meat-eating marsupials look a lot like mice, they are actually very different. All marsupials have one thing in common—how their babies are born. Most other *mammals* grow inside their mothers for a long time and are born fully formed. Baby marsupials grow inside their mothers for only a short time, usually just a few weeks to a month.

When a baby marsupial is born, it is tiny, naked, and blind. Using only instinct and its sense of smell, it crawls through the thick fur of its mother's belly until it reaches the opening of her pouch. This pouch is usually a snug sack, but it is sometimes only a flap of skin. The newborn crawls inside this pouch and attaches its mouth to its mother's *mammary*

Newborn dusky antechinus

gland for a few months. The tiny marsupial drinks its mother's milk and grows until it is big enough to leave its mother's pouch.

This northern quoll is eating a gecko.

Marsupials in the order dasyuromorphia have a trait that sets them apart from other marsupials. Meat-eating marsupials hunt and kill their own food to survive. They have sharp *canine teeth* that they use to kill their *prey*, and their strong *molars* help them slice and chew the meat. Many of them can run quickly and jump high too. This helps them catch animals that are trying to escape.

All dasyuromorphian marsupials live in Australia and on Tasmania, an island south of Australia. They sleep and hunt in many different *habitats*—deserts, grassy plains, and thick, damp forests. So, if you ever visit Australia, keep your eyes and ears open and you just might see a meat-eating marsupial.

The Order of Living Things

A tiger has more in common with a house cat than with a daisy. A true bug is more like a butterfly than a jellyfish. Scientists arrange living things into groups based on how they look and how they act. A tiger and a house cat belong to the same group, but a daisy belongs to a different group.

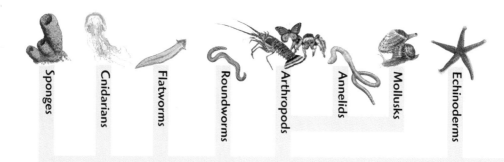

Sponges · Cnidarians · Flatworms · Roundworms · Arthropods · Annelids · Mollusks · Echinoderms

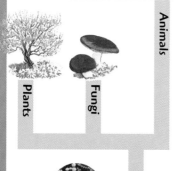

Plants · Fungi · Animals

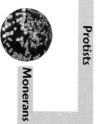

Monerans · Protists

All living things can be placed in one of five groups called *kingdoms*: the plant kingdom, the animal kingdom, the fungus kingdom, the moneran kingdom, or the protist kingdom. You can probably name many of the creatures in the plant and animal kingdoms. The fungus kingdom includes mushrooms, yeasts, and molds. The moneran and protist kingdoms contain thousands of living things that are too small to see without a microscope.

8

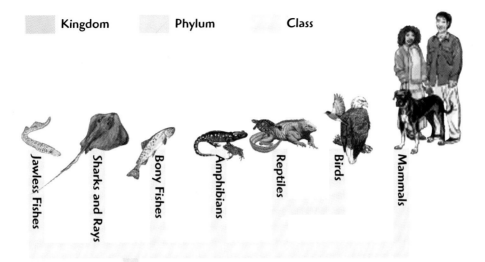

Kingdom   Phylum   Class

Jawless Fishes

Sharks and Rays

Bony Fishes

Amphibians

Reptiles

Birds

Mammals

Chordates

Because there are millions and millions of living things on Earth, some of the members of one kingdom may not seem all that similar. The animal kingdom includes creatures as different as tarantulas and trout, jellyfish and jaguars, salamanders and sparrows, elephants and earthworms.

To show that an elephant is more like a jaguar than an earthworm, scientists further separate the creatures in each kingdom into more specific groups. The animal kingdom can be divided into nine *phyla*. Humans belong to the chordate phylum. All chordates have a backbone.

Each phylum can be subdivided into many *classes*. Humans, mice, and elephants all belong to the mammal class. Each class can be further divided into orders; orders into *families*, families into *genera*, and genera into *species*. All members of a species are very similar.

How Meat-eating Marsupials Fit In

You can probably guess that meat-eating marsupials belong to the animal kingdom. They have more in common with bees and bats than with maple trees and morning glories.

Meat-eating marsupials belong to the chordate phylum. Almost all chordates have a backbone and a skeleton. Can you think of other chordates? Examples include lions, mice, snakes, birds, fish, and whales. The chordate phylum can be divided into a number of classes. Meat-eating marsupials belong to the mammal class. Mice, whales, dogs, cats, and humans are all mammals.

There are twenty-eight different orders of mammals. The meat-eating marsupials make up one of them. They are different from other marsupials because they eat meat and have claws and teeth suited to hunting and eating prey.

There are three different families of meat-eating marsupials. These families contain several different genera and species. You will learn more about fourteen species of meat-eating marsupials in this book.

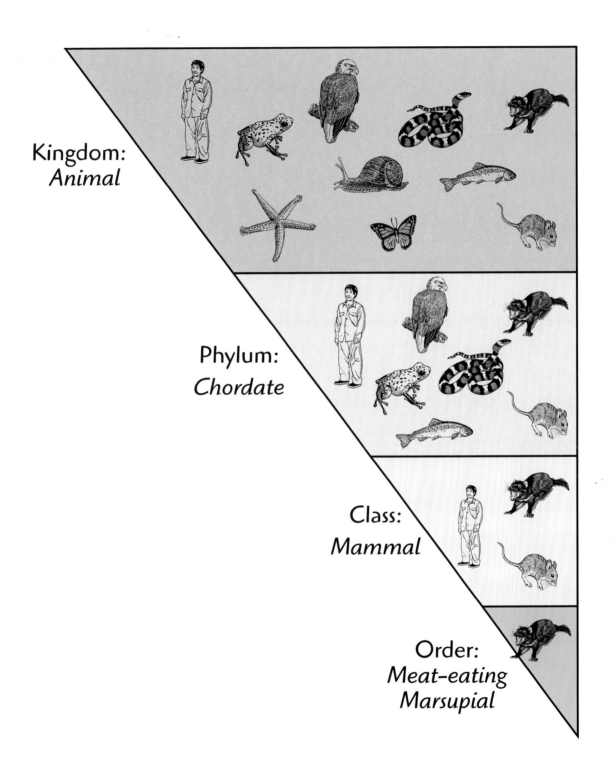

Kingdom: *Animal*

Phylum: *Chordate*

Class: *Mammal*

Order: *Meat-eating Marsupial*

Numbats

FAMILY: Myrmecobiidae
EXAMPLE: Numbat
GENUS AND SPECIES: *Myrmecobius fasciatus*
SIZE: 7 to 11 inches (18 to 28 cm)

A numbat is busy tearing apart a rotting log with its long, sharp claws. Inside are hundreds of squirming termites. The numbat pokes in its slender, sticky tongue. Then it pulls it back, covered with juicy termites. With the help of its strong claws and 4-inch (11-cm) tongue, a numbat has no trouble finding food. This small, striped creature can eat up to 20,000 termites a day! Some people call it a marsupial anteater.

Numbats spend the day wandering through the forest in search of food. They tear open logs and termite mounds, and then they gobble up any termites or ants they find inside. Sometimes they take breaks to bask in the warm Australian sun. When night falls, they crawl into shallow burrows or hollow logs. They curl up in cozy nests made of leaves and grass.

Although female numbats don't have pouches, their belly fur is so thick that it protects their

12

babies almost as well. After growing only 1 month inside their mother, baby numbats are born tiny, blind, and hairless. Each newborn finds a mammary gland and attaches its mouth there for 4 months. The babies are protected only by their mother's dense, shaggy fur. Soon the babies are big enough to stay in the nest while their mother hunts for food. When a numbat is 7 months old, it is finally ready to survive on its own.

Quolls

FAMILY: Dasyuridae
COMMON EXAMPLE: Tiger quoll
GENUS AND SPECIES: *Dasyurus maculatus*
SIZE: 13 1/2 inches (34 cm)

A group of young tiger quolls plays in the thick undergrowth of an Australian rain forest. They wrestle, chase, and stalk each other among the dense leaves and vines. At 3 months, these quolls already have the unique spotted fur—all the way down to their tail tips—that makes them different from other quolls. By the time they are 6 months old, they will be ready to survive on their own.

Tiger quolls sleep, hunt, and play in the dense, wet forests of Australia and Tasmania. They hunt all night and catch anything from bandicoots to small wallabies. Birds, lizards, fish, and even human garbage are all tasty treats for these cat-sized quolls. Special ridged pads on their feet help them climb trees to snag unlucky opossums and gliders. During the day, they curl up in caves or hollow logs to sleep away the long, hot hours.

Male tiger quolls live with females and their young in small family groups. They hiss and spit at any intruders as they fiercely defend their homes. They may be small, but with their strong jaws and sharp teeth, tiger quolls can scare any enemy away!

Antechinus

FAMILY: Dasyuridae
EXAMPLE: Southern dibbler
GENUS AND SPECIES: *Parantechinus apicalis*
SIZE: 9 inches (23 cm)

A southern dibbler darts through the tangled underbrush of the forest floor. With its small body and scurrying feet, it can move quickly and quietly through the thick leaves. It's a swift and silent hunter—it sneaks up on the small creatures it likes to eat. From crunchy insects to slithery lizards, a dibbler can find all the food it needs among the bushes and fallen leaves of the forest.

Because of their white-freckled fur and mouselike appearance, southern dibblers are also called freckled marsupial mice or freckled antechinus. However, they are not real mice. Southern dibblers are meat-eaters just like their marsupial relatives. Most active at dawn and dusk, they root through the underbrush in search of insects, lizards, and small mammals. Sometimes they even climb trees to snag an unlucky bird.

Dibblers meet only during their mating season in March and April. A month and a half later, about eight young are born to each mother. The tiny babies stay in their mother's shallow pouch. They drink her milk and grow until they are big enough to come out. After a few months more, they scamper off into the forest to live and hunt by themselves.

Phascogales
FAMILY: Dasyuridae
COMMON EXAMPLE: Brush-tailed phascogale
GENUS AND SPECIES: *Phascogale tapoatafa*
SIZE: 6 to 8 inches (15 to 20 cm)

Thump! Thump! Thump! As a brush-tailed phascogale drums its forefeet against a tree trunk, the long hairs on its tail stand straight up. This sound tells other phascogales, "Watch out! Danger!" The hungry fox below will have to go somewhere else to find food.

Despite their many enemies, these small, tree-dwelling marsupials are not only prey. They are *predators* too. All night, they scamper along branches and up tree trunks in search of yummy creatures. A phascogale can make a meal out of anything from wriggly spiders to furry mice.

Phascogales are most at home in the treetops of Australian forests. A clawless toe on each hind foot helps them climb quickly and easily through the branches. Their back feet can also twist all the way around so they can clamber down tree trunks headfirst. All the better to catch tasty lizards!

Except during mating season, brush-tailed phascogales live alone. They hunt all night, but when daylight comes, they curl up in cozy nests made of leaves and twigs. Safe in these treetop beds, they sleep the long day away and wait for night to come again.

Tasmanian Devils

FAMILY: Dasyuridae
COMMON EXAMPLE: Tasmanian devil
GENUS AND SPECIES: *Sarcophilus harrisii*
SIZE: 20 to 31 inches (50 to 79 cm)

Night has fallen in a Tasmanian forest. A Tasmanian devil emerges from its underground burrow, and it hungrily sniffs the air. With its bare nose and ears, its long hairless tail, and its broad black-furred body, this marsupial looks like an odd cross between a black bear cub and an overgrown rat. It lumbers off into the trees and follows its nose in search of food.

Because of their bloodcurdling screams and powerful sharp-toothed jaws, Tasmanian devils have earned a reputation for being very fierce. However, Tasmanian devils are not as vicious as some people think. They will defend themselves ferociously, but much of what they eat is already dead—from beached fish to cow carcasses. When they hunt prey, wallabies and wombats are their most common victims. Tasmanian devils also will eat birds, insects, snakes, and even some plants.

Although most Tasmanian devils live alone, they will sometimes share their *territory* with one another. When they find a large carcass, they gather to feed together. Then Tasmanian devils are a noisy bunch. They snort, bark, growl, and scream as they jostle one another and show their teeth. They never actually hurt each other, though, and each one leaves with its belly full.

Antechinus

FAMILY: Dasyuridae
COMMON EXAMPLE: Dusky antechinus
GENUS AND SPECIES: *Antechinus swainsonii*
SIZE: 6 to 7 inches (15 to 18 cm)

A dusky antechinus sleeps in a cozy, leafy nest on the forest floor. It is daytime, and this marsupial is hiding from the hot, bright sun. Once evening comes, however, it will wake up hungry and ready to hunt.

The dusky antechinus is a small mouselike marsupial with dark "dusky" fur. Although it may look tiny and harmless, it is really a fierce hunter. It feeds on all kinds of insects. It catches them with its little paws and crunches them up with its sharp teeth. It swallows worms and hunts lizards among the thick leaves of the forest floor. If a dusky antechinus is lucky, it will even bring down a small bird or two.

These marsupials live alone most of the year. However, they meet during the winter to mate. Males fight one another fiercely for females— but at a high cost. After they mate, most of the males die. Who knows why? Perhaps they are

22

worn out by all the fighting. They also don't eat at all during mating season.

Like all other marsupials, a baby antechinus is born tiny, naked, and blind. After about 8 weeks of drinking its mother's milk in her safe pouch, a young antechinus is big enough to stay alone in the nest. When it is only 3 months old, this little marsupial is ready to live on its own.

Quolls

FAMILY: Dasyuridae
EXAMPLE: Chuditch
GENUS AND SPECIES: *Dasyurus geoffroii*
SIZE: 13 to 14 1/2 inches (33 to 37 cm)

In the cool evening, four young chuditches crawl out of their mother's den. Noses sniffing the air curiously, they scamper through the dead leaves on the forest floor. After 9 weeks in their mother's pouch and 7 more spent snuggled in her den, these little chuditches are ready to run around! By the time they are 6 months old, they will be big enough to take care of themselves.

Chuditches, or western quolls, are short-tailed, big-eared creatures with thick white-spotted fur. They live alone in hollow logs, rock piles, or dens they dig themselves. At night, they scurry through the forest in search of food. In spring and summer, they scratch through the leaves as they look for tasty termites, beetles, and centipedes. If a moth or a gnat flies by, they grab it out of the air with their paws and gobble it up. During fall and winter, they hunt for bigger prey such as rabbits, mice, and bandicoots. Birds, frogs, and lizards are also food for this hungry marsupial.

Chuditches eat what they can, when they can. They can devour a lot of food all at once, just in case they won't be able to eat again for a while. They can also get enough water from the meat of their prey so they don't have to drink often. Chuditches know how to survive!

Tasmanian Wolves

FAMILY: Thylacinidae
EXAMPLE: Tasmanian wolf
GENUS AND SPECIES: *Thylacinus cynocephalus*
SIZE: 44 inches (1.12 m)

A Tasmanian wolf chases a wallaby through the dark forest. Jogging steadily and tirelessly, it pursues the wallaby for a long time. Finally, it gives one last spurt of speed and pounces! One quick, deep bite with its wide jaws, and the wallaby is dead. The Tasmanian wolf drinks the wallaby's blood thirstily before eating the meat.

Because of their wolflike heads and sixteen tiger-like stripes, these large marsupials are called either Tasmanian wolves or Tasmanian tigers. They sleep during the day in hollow logs or rock piles. Sometimes they emerge to bask in the warm sun. When night falls, they come out to hunt. Tasmanian wolves feed mostly on small kangaroos and wallabies. They hunt other animals only when they have to.

Tasmanian wolves usually live alone, but sometimes they hunt in small groups. They talk to each other in many different ways. They bark, growl, or whine to attract attention.

Most people think Tasmanian wolves are extinct. (The photo-graph shown on this page is a stuffed Tasmanian wolf.) The last living one was seen about 65 years ago. However, some footprints have been found that might have been made by a Tasmanian wolf. So maybe somewhere deep in the thick rain forests of Tasmania, these creatures may still survive.

Dunnarts

FAMILY: Dasyuridae
COMMON EXAMPLE: Fat-tailed dunnart
GENUS AND SPECIES: *Sminthopsis crassicaudata*
SIZE: 3 to 3 1/2 inches (7.5 to 9 cm) including tail

It is the Australian wet season, and there are plenty of insects to feed a hungry fat-tailed dunnart. It munches on grasshoppers, beetles, moths, and spiders. The base of its tail slowly swells with fat cells. When the dry season comes, this fattened tail is like a storeroom filled with food for the winter. When the dunnart can no longer find enough to eat, its body lives off of this stored fat. Gradually, its tail shrinks again. The rainy season and a new crop of insects come just in time!

Fat-tailed dunnarts live together in small groups. When a female gives birth, however, she goes off alone with her babies until they are full grown. A female dunnart will breed and raise *litters* one after another for up to 6 months if there is enough food to feed them. If there are not enough insects to eat, these dunnarts may go into a sort of half-sleep to conserve energy.

Like many other meat-eating marsupials, fat-tailed dunnarts are small and mouselike. But don't let that fool you. When night falls, dunnarts are ready to hunt. They spread out into the darkness in search of all the fluttering moths and crunchy beetles they can find.

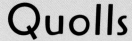

Quolls

FAMILY: Dasyuridae
COMMON EXAMPLE: Eastern quoll
GENUS AND SPECIES: *Dasyurus viverrinus*
SIZE: 18 inches (46 cm)

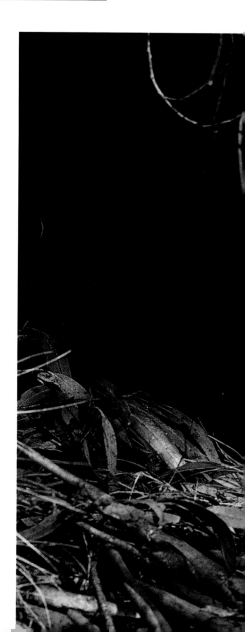

Ears folded snugly against its head, an eastern quoll sleeps curled up in a hollow log. When the sun sets, it wakes up and sniffs the air with its small, mouselike nose. It has been sleeping all day, and now it's time for breakfast. The quoll scrambles out of its nest and scurries off into the forest in search of food.

Eastern quolls are small marsupials with white-spotted fur. When they are hungry, they catch insects, frogs, opossums, and other small animals. A hunting quoll stalks its prey slowly before darting forward and springing onto it. One deep bite to the back of the head finishes off the unlucky victim, and the quoll's hunger will soon be satisfied.

Although rare on the Australian mainland, eastern quolls are fairly common on Tasmania. They usually live alone and change dens often, even in their small territories. When a female quoll gives birth, her babies share her den after about a month in her pouch.

When a mother quoll moves dens, she carries her babies on her back to their new home. After a while, they leave the nest to tussle and play in the long grass or on the forest floor. Soon these young quolls are ready to survive on their own.

Mulgaras

FAMILY: Dasyuridae
COMMON EXAMPLE: Mulgara
GENUS AND SPECIES: *Dasycercus cristicauda*
SIZE: 5 to 8 1/2 inches (12.5 to 21.5 cm)

It is the hottest part of the day in the Australian desert. Deep in the cool sandy soil, a mulgara sleeps curled up in its underground burrow. Toward evening, it will crawl out to bask in the last thin rays of sun. When night finally falls, it will be hungry and ready to hunt.

Mulgaras may be small, but they are excellent hunters. With one quick dash, they attack and sink their teeth into their victims. Once their prey is dead, they settle down to eat. A mulgara devours its victim from head to tail and turns the skin inside out as it goes. Like most desert animals, mulgaras don't need to drink water. They get all the moisture they need from the lizards, snakes, and mice they eat. For an extra treat, mulgaras catch insects.

Female mulgaras do not have complete pouches. They have special folds of skin that protect their babies when they are born. The tiny newborns drink their mother's milk within these skin folds for 2 months until they are ready to walk on their own. Young mulgaras stay with their mothers until they are 4 months old. Then they wander off to make their own homes in the wide, hot desert.

Kultarrs

FAMILY: Dasyuridae
EXAMPLE: Kultarr
GENUS AND SPECIES: *Antechinomys laniger*
SIZE: 3 to 4 inches (8 to 11 cm)

A kultarr gallops across a dry plain as it chases a lizard it has spied. It pushes off with its long, padded hind feet and springs forward to land on its forefeet. Pushing off and landing over and over, it covers a lot of ground quickly. The lizard won't escape the hungry kultarr!

Kultarrs have large ears, long fine fur, and whiskers all over their faces. They sleep during the day in shady nests. Kultarrs make their beds in hollow logs, bushes, or in burrows dug by other animals. When night comes, they roam across the plains and deserts in search of food. Although kultarrs eat mostly insects, they will hunt any animal small enough for them to catch.

Breeding season for kultarrs is during the Australian winter, from June to August. When a female kultarr is pregnant, small folds of skin on her belly grow to cover her mammary glands. When her tiny babies are born, these folds protect them while they drink her milk. Safe within their mother's dense fur, the baby kultarrs grow fat and healthy. Soon they, too, are ready for life in the harsh deserts and dry grasslands. They gallop off on their padded feet and search for insects, lizards, and their own burrow where they can sleep away the long, hot days.

Kowaris

FAMILY: Dasyuridae
COMMON EXAMPLE: Kowari
GENUS AND SPECIES: *Dasyuroides byrnei*
SIZE: 5 to 7 inches (12.5 to 17.5 cm)

Five young kowaris cling to their mother's furry belly as she scurries through the grass. Although they have already left her cozy pouch, they will continue to drink her milk for a little while longer. After they let go completely, they will either stay behind in the nest or ride around on their mother piggyback-style while she hunts for food. These small, pointy-nosed creatures grow quickly. They can have their own babies by the time they are 10 months old.

Kowaris live in the huge deserts and dry grasslands of central Australia. They dig their own burrows deep into the soil and sleep there to escape the scorching sun. When the air cools, they crawl out—noses twitching and bellies empty. They can run quickly, climb easily, and jump up to 20 inches (50 cm) high. So kowaris have no problem finding food. They eat all kinds of insects, spiders, mice, and lizards. Kowaris even pounce on birds or fearlessly snag scorpions to fill their hungry stomachs.

Most kowaris live alone. They mark their homes with a special scent. When they do meet, however, they have many ways of talking with one another. A hiss, snort, or sharp chatter means that they are angry. Rapid tail twitching means, "Keep away!" When a young kowari makes a grating sound, it's saying, "Help!" Its mother comes scurrying to the rescue.

Quolls

FAMILY: Dasyuridae
COMMON EXAMPLE: Little northern native cat
GENUS AND SPECIES: *Dasyurus hallucatus*
SIZE: 9 to 13 1/2 inches (23 to 34 cm)

Snuffle, snuffle! A little northern native cat pokes its wet nose into a rock pile as it snorts and snuffles. With its excellent sense of smell, it can sniff out all kinds of yummy creatures hiding among the rocks. When it finds one, it will pounce on it quickly and gobble it up.

These native cats have huge appetites and spend most of their time hunting. For big meals, they catch rock rats and lizards. They also eat worms, ants, grasshoppers, and other insects. Little northern native cats will even munch on figs when they find them.

Little northern native cats are the smallest of all the quolls. They may weigh only 2 pounds (1 kg) at most. During the day, they nest in hollow logs or among the rocks as they sleep away the long, hot hours. When darkness comes, they crawl out into the night, awake and hungry.

Although some little northern native cats live in forests along the coast, most live on the rocky plains in certain parts of Australia. Rough pads on their back feet help them climb among the rocks as they sniff out any small creature unlucky enough to get in their way.

Meat-eating Marsupials and People

A southern dibbler can have an impact on humans.

How can a creature as small and shy as a kultarr have any impact on humans? And how can people affect such animals as southern dibblers and quolls?

No matter how small the animal, it will probably affect people in some way. Just about every animal, from the tiniest insect to the biggest elephant, has some sort of impact on humans. In turn, humans have changed the lives of most animals. How?

For hundreds of years, the native people of Australia lived easily side by side with meat-eating marsupials. They made up stories about them and included them in their religions. Some hunted them for food, too, but not enough to have any great impact.

Things began to change when Europeans moved to Australia. Because many of the newcomers were farmers or ranchers, they needed a lot of land in order to survive. They cut down trees, plowed up land, and fenced off plains to make space for their crops, sheep, and cattle.

Unfortunately, this human activity destroyed the homes of many animals. Meat-eating marsupials had to look for new places to live. Many that used to roam freely

People in Australia cut down these trees.

across Australia now live only in certain small parts of the country.

Meat-eating marsupials also had some effect on the Europeans. Once their normal habitats were gone, it was hard to find the wild animals they usually ate. Some of them began to raid poultry farms to replace their lost diet. Of course, this made farmers very angry, because now *their* survival was being threatened. Many farmers began to trap and shoot these animals to protect their chickens. In the mid-1800s, the Australian government even paid people to kill Tasmanian devils, which were thought to be the worst poultry raiders.

A kowari eats a mouse.

However, people are beginning to discover that meat-eating marsupials are not the pests that they seemed to be. They actually seldom hunt chickens. In fact, most of these marsupials are good for farmers. The mice and insects that they eat are big pests that most farmers can do without!

There is another way that Europeans made life hard for meat-eating marsupials. When they arrived in Australia, they brought with them many new animals. Some, such as foxes, dogs, and cats, competed with meat-eating marsupials for food and hunted them too.

Because of the threat from new predators, habitat loss, and trapping, there are far fewer meat-eating marsupials than before. Most are confined to small areas in Australia, while some are now found only in Tasmania. Others, such as the Tasmanian wolf, may have disappeared completely. Some other meat-eating marsupials are also in danger of disappearing. The kultarr, chuditch, numbat, and southern dibbler all are listed as endangered species. This means that if something isn't done, these marsupials could disappear forever!

Now many people are doing something to save these animals. Most of them are protected by laws that make it illegal to kill them. Areas of land have also been set aside as national parks, where these marsupials can live in safety. Some places, such as the Perth Zoo, have even begun breeding programs for animals such as the southern dibbler, numbat, and chuditch. Scientists hope to breed them and release them back into the wild so that they can thrive again.

Despite all the positive ways that people and animals can affect each other, it seems that meat-eating marsupials in Australia have not faired well. Although many people are working hard for their return, there have to be more ways to protect them. Can you think of any?

This numbat lives in the Taronga Zoo in Sydney, Australia.

Words to Know

canine teeth—pointed teeth that meat-eating marsupials use to catch and hold their prey

class—a group of creatures within a phylum that share certain characteristics

dasyuromorphia—the scientific name for the order of meat-eating marsupials

family—a group of creatures within an order that share certain characteristics

genus (plural **genera**)—a group of creatures within a family that share certain characteristics

habitat—the environment where a plant or animal lives and grows

kingdom—one of the five divisions into which all living things are placed: the animal kingdom, the plant kingdom, the fungus kingdom, the moneran kingdom, and the protist kingdom

litter—the name for a newborn group of mammals

mammal—an animal that has a backbone and drinks mother's milk when it is young

mammary gland—the part of a female mammal's body that produces milk for its young

marsupial—a mammal that is born in an early stage of development and grows in its mother's pouch

molar—a back tooth with a broad surface for chewing

order—a group of creatures within a class that share certain characteristics

phylum (plural **phyla**)—a group of creatures within a kingdom that share certain characteristics

predator—an animal that hunts and eats other animals

prey—an animal that is hunted and eaten by another animal

species—a group of creatures within a genus that share certain characteristics. Members of the same species can mate and produce healthy young.

territory—the area of land that an animal claims as its own and defends against rivals

Learning More

Books

Marko, Katherine McGlade. *Pocket Babies*. Danbury, CT: Franklin Watts, 1995.

Paul, Tessa. *Down Under*. New York: Crabtree, 1998.

Preller, James. *In Search of the Real Tasmanian Devil*. New York: Scholastic, 1996.

Williams, Brian and Brenda. *World Book Looks at Australia*. Chicago: World Book, 1998.

Videos

Australia's Improbable Animals. National Geographic Video.

National Geographic's Really Wild Animals: Wonders Down Under. National Geographic Video.

Web Sites

Lone Pine Koala Sanctuary
http://www.koala.net/
This site offers information about and pictures of Australian animals, including meat-eating marsupials.

Tour of Tasmania: Marsupials
http://www.tased.edu.au/tot/fauna/marsupials—text.html
This site focuses on Australia's smallest state and the unique animals that live there, including Tasmanian devils and Tasmanian tigers.

Index

Animal kingdom, 8–11

Australia, 7, 14, 30, 36, 38, 40, 41, 42, 43

Brush-tailed phascogale, 18, *19*

Burrow, 12, 20, 32, 34, 36

Chordate phylum, 9, 10–11

Chuditch, 24, *25*, 43

Claws, 10, 12

Dasyuromorphia, 4, 7

Den, 24, 30, 31

Dusky antechinus, 6, 22–23, *23*

Ears, 20, 24, 30, 34

Eastern quoll, 30–31, *31*

Fat-tailed dunnart, 28, *29*

Feet, 14, 16, 18, 34, 38

Fur, 6, 12, 13, 14, 16, 20, 22, 24, 30, 34

Habitats, 7, 41, 42

Kowari, 36–37, *36–37*

Kultarr, 34, *35*, 40, 43

Little northern native cat, 38, 39

Mammals, 6, 9, 10, 16

Mammary gland, 6, 13, 34

Meat-eating marsupials, 4–5, 10–11

   and people, 40–43

   traits of, 6–7

Mother's milk, 6, 16, 23, 32, 34, 36

Mulgara, *5*, 32, *33*

Nest, 12, 13, 18, 22, 23, 30, 31, 34, 36

Numbat, *5*, 12–13, *13*, 43, *43*

Pouch, 6, 12, 16, 23, 24, 31, 32, 36

Predator, 18, 42

Prey, 7, 10, 18, 20, 24, 30, 32

Rain forest, 14, 27

Skin, 4, 6, 32, 34

Southern dibbler, 14, *15*, 40, *40*, 43

Tail, 14, 18, 20, 24, 28, 32, 37

Tasmania, 7, 14, 27, 30, 42

Tasmanian devil, *5*, 20–21, *20–21*, 41

Tasmanian wolf, 26–27, *26–27*, 42

Teeth, 7, 10, 14, 21, 22, 32

Tiger quoll, 14, *15*

About the Author

Erin Pembrey Swan studied animal behavior, literature, and early childhood education at Hampshire College in Massachusetts. She also studied literature and history at University College Galway in Ireland. Her poetry has been published in *The Poet's Gallery: The Subterraneans* and *The Poet's Gallery: Voices of Selene* in Woodstock, New York, and *The Cuirt Journal* in Galway, Ireland. Ms. Swan is also the author of *Land Predators Around the World*, *Primates: From Howler Monkeys to Humans*, *Land Predators of North America*, *Camels and Pigs: What They Have in Common*, and *Kangaroos and Koalas: What They Have in Common*. Although she lives in New York City, Ms. Swan spends a great deal of time traveling.